MW01641471

Table of Contents

Unreasonable Boss? 8 Ways to Honor Yourself in a Toxic Workplace

"Good bosses care about getting important things done. Exceptional bosses care about their people." ~Jeff Haden

"I'll need you to log your work down to the minute on this spreadsheet," she said pointing to my computer where an elaborate timesheet was swallowing up my entire screen.

I looked up at her, confused—nope, more like utterly stunned. Was she for real? My body seemed to know before my mind that I'd just entered some sort of workplace twilight zone.

I had a sinking feeling in my gut, and it was sounding some sort of alarm deep in my chest, making my heart do somersaults. She was serious. Clearly the shock was holding my throat hostage because all I could muster was a single word...

"Okay," I replied quietly, and off she went, oblivious to the impact her passive aggressive requests were having on me.

I had just returned to work from maternity leave, and with three children aged six and under at home, I needed some flexibility in my work schedule.

I was clocking in while it was still dark outside, long before anyone else so I could get home to my little ones with enough time for quality cuddles before tucking them in for the night.

I was trying to achieve motherhood level 100 while still trying to conquer my career. Did I mention I was also pursuing my second master's degree?

Yes, I was on a mission to prove that I could still do it all.

Of course, I knew "doing it all" was the age-old battle of every modern woman trying to be equal parts supermum and Sheryl Sandberg, but despite my husband's very real concerns, I was doing it all.

In fact, I was working harder, longer, and smarter than most people in my department because, like most mothers returning to work, I had that unshakable guilt inside telling me that I had to prove I was bringing my very best and not taking advantage of my "mum status."

So when my new line manager insisted on tracking my every move, decision, and waking moment I was utterly confused. I mean, there I was, delivering the project deliverables and meeting each and every deadline, and her biggest worry was that she wasn't squeezing every possible work minute out of me?

So, I did what so many of us do to prove our value to a superior: I went above and beyond to show her I was worthy of my pay no matter what it took. But the more I gave, the more she pushed, until finally, late one night, after yet another night of venting to my poor, put-upon husband, I found myself sprawled out on my living room floor, no longer able to hold back the tears.

I was broken like a shattered glass. I realized that I had allowed her constant micromanaging to bring me to the brink, and that no matter what I did, she was never going to stop.

My health was suffering. My relationships were suffering. I was suffering. I went from optimistic, happy, and loving my job to moody, stressed, and miserable. I dreaded going into this space where I never felt good enough.

Work had begun to feel like a torture chamber. A place where the person charged with helping me succeed at my job was slowly but methodically chipping away at my confidence, and it was spilling over into my personal life.

I finally accepted the reality: I had allowed her actions to steal my joy, and it was breaking my heart with every passing day. I felt so defeated.

It became very clear to me that she didn't seem to trust me, and seemed to like me even less. I was at a loss for what to do, but I knew that I couldn't survive in this environment for much longer, so I had to figure something out.

I went on a mission to remove the poison that had engulfed my workplace experience and bring the light back into my life. Because the truth was that in that moment I couldn't leave my job. For now, at least, I had to deal with her and I had to find a way to cope, no matter what.

So I went on a journey to figure out what I could do to honor myself and my happiness, because as far as I was concerned, suffering was completely optional.

I had a family that needed me to get back to the old me. And frankly, I needed that too. I needed to survive my unreasonable boss. I'm guessing if you're reading this, you have your own unreasonable boss whose overwhelming negative energy is causing problems in your life.

I'm here to share with you the eight tools I used to get through one of the hardest times in my life so you can conquer your own "horrible boss."

1. Find your community and ask for help.

Dealing with an unreasonable boss sometimes takes an army, or in my case a community, to survive.

The truth is with any toxic relationship, whether it's your boss or someone else, you go through a period of wondering, "Wait, am I just absolutely crazy that I feel this way? Is it all in my head? Am I silly for letting this mess with my emotions?"

I needed someone to give me perspective. Someone safe who would give me the space to explore, without judgment, what I was feeling–an objective observer who could reflect back to me what I was really experiencing.

What's interesting is that even when you feel all alone, you'll often find that you're still surrounded by amazing people willing to help you weather the storm. I found that safety net in friends, family, and colleagues, in and outside of work, who were all willing to lend an ear.

They were quite incredible really, offering advice and helping me figure out where things may have gone wrong. They allowed me to express my anger, frustration, and even let me cry. More than anything, though, they were objective and honest with me, gently leading me toward making the right moves for dealing with my boss.

In their own unique ways, all of these people were empathetic and supportive. They were the break in the ocean keeping these waves of intensity from knocking me out cold.

If you are at a loss for whom to turn toward, though, you can always turn inward. Journal about what you're experiencing. Journaling often allows us to work through our issues on the page. And, of course, there are always tons of wonderful mental health professionals who can help give you a safe space to talk.

2. Make relaxing rituals a part of your "job."

Being in a workplace with such high-pressure demands meant I was under a lot of stress. Sadly, there were days that I found myself bringing my boss's energy home with me. The conflicts of the day ran wild through my mind, and the fear of not meeting my boss's demands left me in constant flight or fight mode.

My anxiety was high. I knew that I needed to create rituals that would help me break away from work and make my free time mine again. Because here's the thing: Our wind-down time is when our minds and bodies recalibrate and restore, which is especially important when you've spent eight hours in a toxic work environment.

In fact, I came to think of relaxing as a part of my job like meeting a deadline or completing a daily task. Because relaxation can do so much for honoring your health, including lowering blood pressure and heart rate, reducing anxiety, and improving mild depression.

For me, a long warm bath was my me-time. But relaxation can come in so many forms: reading, yoga, a brisk walk, listening to your favorite Adele tune, watching a hilarious comedy, meditation, mindfulness, T'ai Chi, Chi Kung, or even spending time laughing with loved ones.

Whatever it is, make it a big part of your self-care routine, and you'll start to preserve your sanity in the midst of your workplace chaos.

3. Let physical activity soothe and re-energize you.

While I was dealing with my manager, there was one thing that helped me release all of the extra adrenaline I had running through my body: running.

Throwing on my sneakers and hitting a long path lined with big, beautiful trees was one of my favorite things to do. Not only was it another form of relaxing me-time, it released the endorphins that I was desperately in need of at this time.

Endorphins are feel-good hormones, released through physical activity, that elevate our moods. Hacking into your happy chemicals with exercise is an incredible way to combat a stressful work environment.

Physical activity can be any number of things: dancing, trampoline jumping, cycling, baseball, skateboarding, or just simply going for a run. If you can find a community to do this with, like a team or running group, even better!

4. Focus on the big picture of abundance.

It's true that the little things remind us how insignificant some of the tougher things in our lives are.

Have you ever stared out at the stars on a quiet night and for a brief moment remembered how truly tiny you are in this great big universe? It’s in those moments that we’re reminded that the harmful energy of one bad boss, in the grand scheme of things, is really insignificant.

We realize that it’s only a blip in our long lives on this earth, and that knowledge and perspective brought me peace.

Finding these types of moments in our lives is so crucial. It can be found in so many unexpected places and moments. For me, I found it with my loved ones—my wonderful husband, six-year-old giggly daughter, four-year-old full-of-beans son, and two-year-old love-bug baby girl. They all kept me busy and grounded and reminded me that work was such a small part of this amazing life I was leading.

There were other parts of my life that deserved my attention and energy as well, and that reminder helped me re-center over and over again.

There are so many things that can bring these awe-inspiring moments fully into focus during a difficult work phase in your life: volunteering with those less fortunate; creative outlets like painting, sewing, or cooking, camping; or any activity that brings you into nature. These are not only distractions from a difficult work environment, but also reminders that life is fun, beautiful, and worthy of your attention.

5. Feed your calm, not your stress.

Dealing with a passive-aggressive, micro-managing boss meant not only dealing with a lot of stress, but also with tons of anxiety. And with lots of anxiety, sometimes my automatic reaction was to self-soothe with Ben & Jerry's.

Yes, I know we've all been there, that point of utter disappointment where all we can think to do is dive headfirst into the cookie jar.

This is where being a health professional helps. I knew using food to manage my stress and deal with my emotional issues would be a slippery slope. On top of that, foods like ice cream and cookies would only make my plummeting moods worse.

Here's the thing: a sugary snack or baked goodie will send your blood sugar on a wild rollercoaster, which will further negatively affect your stress, anxiety, and depression. I was already dealing with one mood-enhancing rollercoaster (my boss!) I didn't need to make things worse with my diet.

I made a plan to eat in a way that supported my stress relief by eating foods that kept my blood sugar on an even keel. I incorporated whole grain products like brown rice, protein, and berries, and avoided stimulants like caffeine, alcohol, and nicotine, which could make mood swings worse.

I also increased my omega-3 intake, which has been proven to reduce feelings of sadness, pessimism, indifference, sleeplessness, and low libido. You can find omega-3s in some pretty yummy foods like seafood, walnuts, flaxseed, and leafy green vegetables.

6. Worship at the altar of sleep, because it's sacred.

With three kids, and a fourth in the form of a grouchy boss, I spent many sleepless nights stressed out. My mind would be constantly racing. The more I lost sleep, the worse things would be for me the next day.

I grew more and more irritable and angry, and was just plain exhausted, which meant going to work the next morning to face my boss was getting more difficult.

Lack of sleep meant my filters were down, and my ability to balance my mood was completely compromised. Basically, no sleep = falling into a spiral of self-loathing even at the smallest criticism from a difficult boss.

"Switching off" the stress to get a good night's sleep can be difficult, but making it a priority can make the difference between a good day or a bad day at work.

A few things that help include trying to keep a regular sleep cycle (sleeping and waking at the same time every day) and avoiding stimulating activities before bed like TV, tablets, computers, or phones. The light given off by these devices suppress melatonin, which supports sleep.

You can also include a night-time routine that helps you get into a relaxed state, like an end of day warm bath, a massage from your partner, aromatherapy, or a night-time meditation that lets you release tension.

7. Take a step back and handle what's yours.

When we're in a difficult circumstance like I was with my boss, we can spend a lot of time in our heads trying to figure it all out. I would always wonder, "Did I do something to cause this? Could I have done something differently?"

The reality was that I could keep spinning my wheels trying to figure it out, but not everything was in my control. I learned to take a step back, reflect, and objectively look at the situation. I identified the real stressors I was facing, and then I went about the business of figuring out what was in my control and what wasn't.

What wasn't in my control I accepted and tried my best to let go of, but what was in my control I approached head on.

I looked at whether or not my coping strategies were effective and whether any strategies from past experiences could be modified to fit this situation. I also kept a close eye on my self-talk. It's so incredibly easy to fall into negative self-talk, but I made it my mission to be kind to myself. I gave myself plenty of positive pep talks and pats on the back for any small victory.

Make sure that you are doing the same to help combat stressful situations.

8. Make the right moves, confidently.

Ultimately, your happiness and health should always at the top of your priority list. If you can't deal with the situation with your difficult boss using any of the above, then it's time to deal with the problem in the healthiest way possible.

In my case, I did everything I could to remedy the situation on my own, by explaining to my boss the impact her behavior was having on me and by going through grievance channels at work, which meant mediation with my boss through Human Resources, for example. But in the end, I knew that staying in the situation was causing too much harm.

When the opportunity came up to take voluntary redundancy, I jumped at it, and I spent some time with my family while I figured out my next steps. Building an exit strategy that puts you first is always something to applaud. Sometimes, the healthiest thing we can do for ourselves doesn't look like the most practical, but it'll save us years of heartache, stress, and ultimately, bad health.

—

These eight strategies helped me move through a toxic environment with a little more ease. What I came to find out, though, was that my boss was dealing with some of her own stress that she was bringing to the workplace. She was projecting her personal problems onto me, the mother with three children who seemed to "have it all."

She was roping me into carrying the burden of her issues in these micro-aggressions of control she was laying on me. Because of this, the truth is, I was never going to win her over, and I'd venture to guess that whatever is pushing your boss to keep you down is something you may never be able to fix either. Just remember that you are not required to carry someone else's baggage.

Your health matters, which is why I hope these tips help you find peace and health on your journey.

10 Brilliant Tips for Dealing With a Difficult Boss

In an ideal world, we would all have fantastic managers—bosses who helped us succeed, who made us feel valued, and who were just all-around great people.

Unfortunately, that's not always the case. But, whether the person you work for is a micromanager, has anger management problems, shows favoritism toward one person, is a flat-out workplace bully, or just isn't very competent, you still have to make the best of the situation and get your job done.

To help out, we've gathered the best advice from around the web for dealing with a bad boss. Try one or more of these tips to find some common ground with your boss—or at least stay sane until you find a new gig.

1. Make Sure You’re Dealing With a "Bad Boss"

Before trying to fix your bad boss, make sure you really are dealing with one. Is there a reason for her behavior, or are you being too hard on him or her?

"Observe your boss for a few days and try to notice how many things she does well versus poorly. When she is doing something "bad," try to imagine the most forgiving reason why it could have occurred. Is it truly her fault, or could it be something out of her control?"

2. Identify Your Boss' Motivation

Understanding why your boss does or cares about certain things can give you insight into his or her management style.

"...if the rules are totally out of control, try to figure out your boss' motivation. Maybe it's not that he really cares about how long your lunch break takes; he actually cares about how it looks to other employees and their superiors."

3. Don't Let it Affect Your Work

No matter how bad your boss' behavior, avoid letting it affect your work. You want to stay on good terms with other leaders in the company (and keep your job!).

"Don't try to even the score by working slower, or taking excessive 'mental health' days or longer lunches. It will only put you further behind in your workload and build a case for your boss to give you the old heave-ho before you're ready to go."

4. Stay One Step Ahead

Especially when you're dealing with a micromanager, head off your boss' requests by anticipating them and getting things done before they come to you.

"...a great start to halting micromanagement in its tracks is to anticipate the tasks that your manager expects and get them done well ahead of time. If you reply, 'I actually already left a draft of the schedule on your desk for your review,' enough times, you'll minimize the need for her reminders. She'll realize that you have your responsibilities on track—and that she doesn't need to watch your every move."

5. Set Boundaries

Working with someone who seems to have no boundaries means that you have to go ahead and set them.

"One of the challenges of unlikable people is that they come with equally unlikable behavior—and it's important to learn how to distance yourself from that behavior. As Robert Frost said, 'Good fences make good neighbors.'"

6. Stop Assuming They Know Everything

Just because someone has a managerial title doesn't mean that they have all the right answers, all the time.

"I realized then that, just because someone is in a position of authority, doesn't mean he or she knows everything. From that point forward, I stopped assuming the title 'manager was equivalent to 'all knowing.'

7. Act as the Leader

When dealing with an incompetent boss, sometimes it's best to make some leadership decisions on your own.

If you know your area well enough, there is no reason to not go ahead creating and pursuing a direction you know will achieve good results for your company. People who do this are naturally followed by their peers as an informal leader. Management, although maybe not your direct boss, will notice your initiative. Of course, you don't want to do something that undermines the boss, so keep him or her in the loop.

8. Identify Triggers

If your boss has anger management problems, identify what triggers her meltdowns and be extra militant about avoiding those.

"For example, if your editor flips when you misspell a source's name, be sure to double and triple-check your notes. And if your boss starts foaming at the mouth if you arrive a moment after 8 AM, plan to get there at 7:45—Every. Single. Day."

9. Use Tips from Couples' Therapy

When dealing with disagreement, pull on some tenants from couple's therapy to work through the issue.

"Simply repeat back to him what he said and ask "Is that what you meant?" (a standard trick ripped from couples' therapy). If he agrees to your recap, ask him to tell you more about it. When you repeat someone's perspective back to him, you give him a chance to expound and, crucially, to feel heard."

10. Avoid Future Bad Bosses

When interviewing with a new company, do your research ahead of time to make sure you're not getting into another situation with a less-than-ideal manager.

"Have coffee or lunch with one or more staffers at the new company. Ostensibly, your purpose is to learn general information about the company and its culture. However, use this opportunity to discover as much about your potential boss as possible, without appearing creepy, of course."

7 Ways To Deal With A Difficult Boss

It's the age-old dilemma: you've finally found the ideal job, you're doing work that you love, you like your co-workers...but your boss is insufferable. The ultimate micromanager, and despite your best efforts, you're just not able to forge the sort of positive employee-supervisor relationship you had hoped you'd have in this role.

If this sounds familiar, don't stress too much. And know firsthand that you're not the only person to ever butt heads with your boss—I've had my share of clients who were job searching solely to get away from a boss they didn't like. I'm of the belief that people often want to leave managers, not companies.

Actually, half of the employees in one survey reported leaving a job to get away from their boss. So you're not alone. There are actually many steps you can take to improve the relationship, or, at the very least, smooth things over enough so that your daily work life is tolerable.

1. Assess the situation. Do you have any level of responsibility for the damaged relationship, or does your boss have a negative relationship with everyone at work? Is your boss guilty of bad workplace behaviors in general, or does their beef seem to be directed at you individually? Be honest with yourself about your own potential culpability in the situation. If you're guilty of contributing to the negative dynamic in some way, own it and address it. Ignoring it will only exacerbate the situation.

2. Practice empathy. Contemplate what your boss may be dealing with, either personally or professionally, that may be contributing to how they treat their employees. Are they constantly stressed about tight deadlines? Do they have a difficult boss themselves? If you're comfortable doing so and the right opportunity arises, it might even help to ask your boss to open up about what they're dealing with. Putting yourself in their shoes can help you understand their perspective and allow you to be more sympathetic about their circumstances and behaviors.

3. **Be tactful.** I normally encourage my clients to be open and honest in their communications at work, but with a delicate situation like this, it's important to think things through carefully before you speak. Saying the wrong thing at the wrong time when tensions are running high risks making the situation much, much worse than it already is.So choose your words carefully, and document your interactions with your boss—having a

solid paper trail will ensure that if the situation does at some point escalate, you've insulated yourself from blame. A key tip is to stay results focused: focus on the behavior as something that's blocking your ability to create results, versus attacking their personality.

4. Vent your frustrations, but not to your colleagues. Dealing with a less-than-stellar boss on the daily can really wear you down. Opening up to a trusted friend or family member can help alleviate some of that stress. Not only will it help you get things off your chest, but they may be able to offer you a different perspective about the situation and what is really going on. And remember… Ask someone whose opinion you have the utmost respect for. The last thing you need is fuel to your fire.

5. Don't burn bridges. You never know when you might need this person as a reference—many prospective employers ask specifically if they can contact your direct supervisor from your previous jobs, and having to respond "no" will raise red flags and will require an awkward explanation.

As difficult as it might be, make sure you don't allow the dynamic to compromise your professional reputation.

6. Try to get transferred to another team or department. If you work for a sizeable company that has other opportunities, look into whether there might be openings on a team that is not supervised by your current boss. This is a great, discreet way of getting a new boss without having to leave the company or have an awkward conversation with HR about your boss's behavior.

7. **Jump ship.** Sometimes, it's just not worth staying if you're that miserable. There's actually evidence that employees who have a strong relationship with their bosses are more engaged at work. So depending on the circumstances, your poor relationship with your boss could be costing you professionally, not to mention the stress it adds to your day-to-day work life.

Ultimately, only you will know the best way to handle the situation. Have a heart-to-heart with yourself. Is the stress and tension of the situation worth it? Is it affecting your work? Or is the negative relationship just a minor drawback to a job that you otherwise love? Listen to yourself before making any abrupt decisions about how to handle the situation. At the end of the day, know that no one deserves to be mistreated at work, and if you do have to move on, your ideal job is out there, one that comes with fulfilling work and a positive, supportive boss.

How to Manage a Micromanaging Boss

Every morning when I arrived at my office, I used to find a to-do list printed out and neatly laid on my keyboard, courtesy of my boss. But this wasn't a typical bulleted list—it was a long (upwards of three pages), drawn-out document, where each bullet point was accompanied by paragraphs of elaboration, laying out to the very smallest of details exactly how I should accomplish the task.

And as I stared at this book (er, document), wondering if it would somehow look less menacing after my morning coffee, I couldn't help but think, Wouldn't it have taken her less time to just complete the things on the list?

And my micromanaging boss didn't stop there—she constantly asked for updates on my progress, added to and modified the list, and ultimately refused to let me do my job on my terms.

For a while, I thought it was impossible to change my boss' overbearing ways without completely offending her (and risking my job!). But over time, I did. And luckily, there are several ways you can show your manager that you're in control—and loosen her grip a little bit, too.

1. Eliminate Any Possibility That She Needs to Micromanage

Once I'd experienced my boss' micromanaging for a few weeks, I assumed there wasn't anything I could do but succumb to it. Since I knew she was going to remind me about my deadlines and check on my progress multiple times a day, I figured there was no reason for me to duplicate her efforts. And while my work was still getting done on time, I couldn't really ignore all those emails titled "Urgent," I was probably sending her the message that I couldn't manage my workload without her so-called "help."

So, first things first: Take a hard look at your recent attitude, productivity, and track record to make sure that you aren't doing anything to solicit such nitpicking. Are you unintentionally (or intentionally) letting your work slip through the cracks? Do you show up late? Miss deadlines? In this case, of course she's going to try to manage every detail—because she's worried that you can't.

2. Anticipate What She Wants—and Act

A lot of the tasks my boss assigned me (and constantly reminded me about) were tasks I knew I was supposed to do—she just wanted to make extra sure that I had them on my radar. It was incredibly frustrating when she'd walk into my office to say, "Hey, I just wanted to remind you that we need to get the weekly schedule emailed out today," when I was already well aware of the assignment. (Seriously, I did it every week.)

So, a great start to halting micromanagement in its tracks is to anticipate the tasks that your manager expects and get them done well ahead of time. If you reply, "I actually already left a draft of the schedule on your desk for your review," enough times, you'll minimize the need for her reminders. She'll realize that you have your responsibilities on track—and that she doesn't need to watch your every move.

3. Provide Updates Proactively

Micromanagers want to be in control—that's why they frequently ask for updates, tell you how to complete tasks, and check in incessantly to make sure that things are going according to schedule. Since they can't actually complete every project themselves (that's why they hired you, after all), micromanaging helps them stay as involved as possible.

To head this off, try proactively sending your manager regular updates, before she has a chance to ask for them. Every morning, pull together an email outlining what you accomplished the day before, what you plan on accomplishing that day, and if you have any questions or need any input. (This is part of managing up, it's key when you're dealing with a bad boss.)

This will serve multiple purposes: First, your boss will know exactly where your current workload stands, staving off her constant questioning. Second, with a quick glance, she'll be able to address your questions, provide input, or suggest ideas in one direct reply—which will help her feel involved, yet prevent her multiple mid-day check-ins.

And third, she'll eventually realize that you're organized and detail-oriented and that you can manage your responsibilities without her constant intervention—so she'll feel comfortable pulling back and giving up the reigns.

4. Use Your Words

When it comes to bosses and their management styles, confrontation doesn't usually seem like a viable option. But in my case, I was working for a friend at a small startup. She always encouraged her employees to bring up issues they were experiencing—even if they concerned the way she ran the business.

So, during one of our one-on-one conversations, I carefully explained that I felt like she didn't trust me with my work. She admitted that she had a hard time delegating and was used to doing everything herself. In short, she couldn't "let go." But she realized the effect it was having on my productivity and happiness, and she promised to make a better effort to step back and let me accomplish my work the way I wanted to.

Obviously, this won't work in every situation. At my current (and much more corporate) job, I wouldn't feel nearly as comfortable confronting my boss about such an issue. However, there are small—and respectful—ways you can express your opinion. For example, ask your boss for the opportunity to complete a small project on your own from start to finish, with the understanding that afterward, you'll discuss what you did well and what you can improve upon next time.

Pose it this way: It'll be a great learning opportunity and a chance for your manager to evaluate your work methods. And if you knock it out of the park, you'll instantly convey that you can work independently of your manager's constant input.

And as you notice differences in behavior, let her know how much you appreciate the hands-off approach: "Thank you for trusting me with this project—having to create the plan and find the right resources on my own really helped me polish my project management skills!"

Shifting your micromanaging boss' management style won't be easy, and it certainly won't be immediate. But if you can show her that you're trustworthy, thorough, and ultimately, on top of your work, you'll be able to inspire that change over time.

Made in United States
Cleveland, OH
02 May 2025